Zoom in on
MINING ROBOTS

Sara L. Latta

Enslow Publishing
101 W. 23rd Street
Suite 240
New York, NY 10011
USA

enslow.com

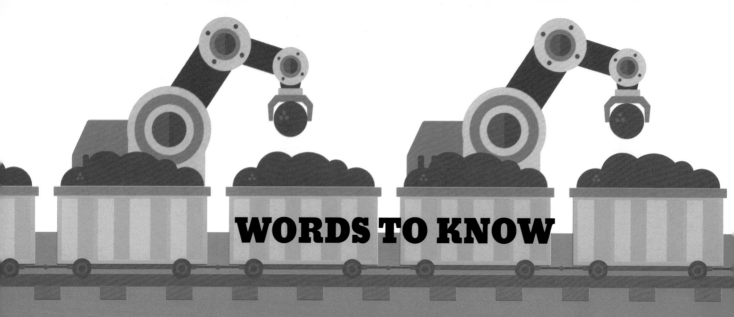

WORDS TO KNOW

asteroid A small rocky body going around the sun.

pollute To put harmful or toxic things into water, air, or soil.

program A set of instructions given to a machine.

robot A machine that can carry out a series of actions by itself.

sensor A part that detects light, temperature, pressure, sound, or motion.

toxic Very harmful; able to cause sickness or death.

CONTENTS

Taking coal out of an underground mine is dangerous work. Robots can make it safer.

Mining Robots

People have been digging useful materials out of the earth for thousands of years. We use stones to make buildings. We heat those buildings with coal from the earth. Metals like iron and copper come from the earth. We get all of these things from the earth by a process called mining.

Miners use machines to dig deep underground. They haul material to the surface. It is a dirty job. It is dangerous. Now,

Robots can make mining safer for people.

mining companies are starting to use robots to do some of that work. They are making mining safer for people.

What Are Robots?

Robots are machines. They can do jobs by themselves. Computers control most robots. The computers tell the robots what to do. Robots have parts that allow the robot to move, grab, turn, or lift. They have sensors like cameras or microphones. The sensors tell the robot about what is nearby.

What's in a Name?

The word "robot" comes from a Czech word. It means "forced work."

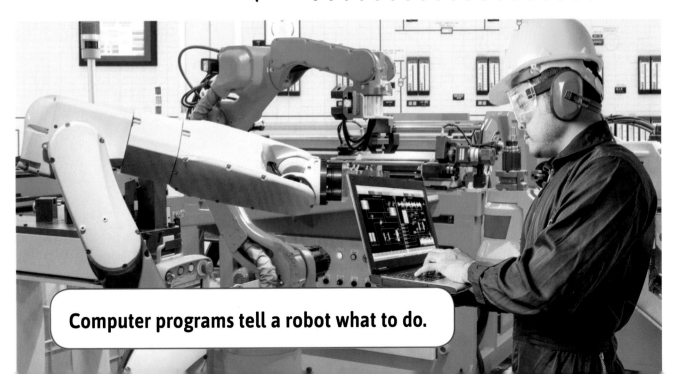

Computer programs tell a robot what to do.

The Future of Land Mining: Robots

Miners drill deep underground to get the materials they need. Robots can do this work. Robots lay bombs in a mine deep underground. The robots set them off from a distance. The bombs blast away at the rock. After the blast, robots move in to make sure the mine walls do not cave in.

One mining company in Australia uses trucks the size of small houses. The trucks carry iron ore out of mines. None of the trucks have drivers. The robot trucks are programmed

Robot trucks never get tired.

to run a certain route around the mines. They are cheaper to run than trucks with drivers. They are faster too.

Mining Safety

Mining companies sometimes need to explore old mines. Mines may release gases that could injure or kill people. They may be filled with toxic mud. Robots inspect old

To the Rescue

When mines cave in, miners can be injured or trapped inside. Researchers are working on a Cave Crawler robot to help rescue trapped miners. The Cave Crawler robot could bring supplies to trapped miners.

A mine is a dangerous place to work. Robots can check old mines before human miners enter.

mines before human miners go in. Robots can help map out the old mines.

Mining often pollutes water nearby. The water is dangerous for living things. It contains lead and other metals. Scientists have made tiny robots to clean up polluted water. Each robot is smaller than the width of a human hair. Thousands of these robots can remove nearly all of the metals from a water sample in just one hour.

Deep-Sea Mining Robots

Metals like copper, gold, and silver are becoming harder to find. We need them for computers and cell phones. We have nearly used up the supply on land. But there is still a rich stock of these and other metals. The stock is miles under the surface of the ocean. Mining companies will soon begin to dig for materials on the ocean floor.

The deep-sea miners will be robots, not humans. Robots will soon begin work off the coast of Papua New Guinea. They

Powerful robots will soon start to look for mineral treasure deep under the sea.

are the size of semitrucks. One uses blades the size of small cars to chew through rocks. The other smashes rock walls into bits. A third robot will pump the crushed rock and water up to a ship above.

Scientists look at pictures sent from an underwater robot.

These three large robots can mine the ocean floor for copper and gold.

How Will Deep-Sea Mining Affect Ocean Life?

Many people are afraid the deep-sea mining will harm fish and other life in the area. Mining would destroy the homes of deep-sea creatures. It could pollute the water. Mining companies are trying to figure out how to protect deep-sea life.

Jewels of the Sea

Many diamonds already come from shallow ocean floor mines off the coast of South Africa.

Mining Robots That Are Out of This World

Earth shares the solar system with other planets and thousands of chunks of rocks. Those rocks are called asteroids. They may be hundreds of miles across. They are a rich source of metals and minerals that we need. Now some companies are planning to send swarms of robots into space. They will check out asteroids for materials. They hope to set up mines on the asteroids. Robots will mine the materials and send them back to Earth.

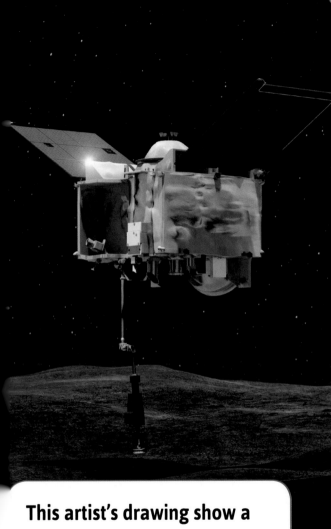

This artist's drawing show a robot taking samples from an asteroid. Some day, more permanent mines might be set up in space.

Robots and Space Travel

If you wanted to send a spaceship to Mars, you would have to pack a lot of supplies on your rocket. You would need enough air, water, and fuel to last the trip. That would cost a lot of money. But what if you could mine the stuff you needed once you get there? You wouldn't have to pack as much stuff on the spaceship.

That is what space scientists think. They are looking at ways to use robots connected to Earth to mine materials in outer space. Space robots would make space travel much cheaper.

NASA's RASSOR robot is strong and built to mine materials on the moon.

NASA's "Swarmie" robots are designed and programmed to hunt for minerals on the moon the way ants hunt.

ACTIVITY:
CREATE A RUBBER BAND RACER

Robot mining trucks haul heavy loads. Now it's time for you to make your own "robot" truck.

What you'll need:

- For the truck's body: the bottom of a small shoe box or cereal box. If using a cereal box, cut off the front to form a wide, shallow body
- Straws
- For the truck's axles: two wooden dowels that fit inside the straws.
- For the truck's wheels: four plastic bottle caps of the same size.
- Rubber bands
- A hot glue gun
- Two small cup hooks

What you'll do:

1. Cut a notch one inch by one inch (2.5 centimeters by 2.5 centimeters) wide at the center of the short end of the truck's body.

2. Make two lengths of straw the same width as the body of the truck. If your truck body is wider than one straw, you can join two straws together by sliding the end of one into the other. Glue or tape the straws across the body of the truck. The straws should be about ½ inch (1 cm) from the ends.

3. Cut the dowels so that each is one inch (2.5 cm) longer than the width of the truck body. Thread the dowels through the straws. These are your axles. Screw a cup hook into the middle of the rear axle.

4. Ask an adult to help you attach the wheels to the axles with a hot glue gun.

5. Screw a small cup hook into the top side of the body of the truck, just behind the front axle.

6. Loop one end of a large rubber band on the hook at the front of the truck. Loop the other over the hook on the rear axle.

7. Your truck is ready to roll! Turn the rear axle several times to wind the rubber band around it. Set the truck on a smooth surface and let it go!

Robot trucks need to haul heavy loads. Try loading your truck with small rocks or coins. How much can your truck carry? Experiment with different kinds of wheels or different sizes and strengths of rubber bands. Will your truck work on bumpy surfaces?

LEARN MORE

Books

Schulman, Mark. *TIME for Kids Explorers: Robots*. New York, NY: TIME for Kids, 2014.

Stewart, Melissa. *National Geographic Readers: Robots*. Washington, DC: National Geographic Children's Books, 2014.

Tuchman, Gail. *Robots*. New York, NY: Scholastic, 2015.

Websites

All About Mining
easyscienceforkids.com/all-about-mining/
Learn some basic facts about mining.

Robotics: Facts
idahoptv.org/sciencetrek/topics/robots/facts.cfm
Check out many interesting facts about robots.

INDEX

Published in 2018 by Enslow Publishing, LLC.
101 W. 23rd Street, Suite 240, New York, NY 10011

Copyright © 2018 by Enslow Publishing, LLC.
All rights reserved.

No part of this book may be reproduced by any means without the written permission of the publisher.

Library of Congress Cataloging-in-Publication Data

Names: Latta, Sara L., author.
Title: Zoom in on mining robots / Sara L. Latta.
Description: New York, NY : Enslow Publishing, [2018] | Includes bibliographical references and index.
Identifiers: LCCN 2017023213 | ISBN 9780766092303 (library bound) | ISBN 9780766094420 (pbk.) | ISBN 9780766094437 (6 pack)
Subjects: LCSH: Mineral industries—Automation—Juvenile literature. | Robotics—Juvenile literature. | Robots, Industrial—Juvenile literature.
Classification: LCC TN148 .L38 2018 | DDC 622.028/4—dc23
LC record available at https://lccn.loc.gov/2017023213

Printed in the United States of America

To Our Readers: We have done our best to make sure all website addresses in this book were active and appropriate when we went to press. However, the author and the publisher have no control over and assume no liability for the material available on those websites or on any websites they may link to. Any comments or suggestions can be sent by email to customerservice@enslow.com.

Photo Credits: Cover, p. 1 Collart Hervé/Sygma/Getty Images; pp. 4, 11 Tyler Stableford/Stone/Getty Images; p. 6 Sputnik/Science Photo Library; p. 7 Suwin/Shutterstock.com; p. 9 Komatsu; pp. 14, 16 Photo courtesy of Nautilus Minerals; p. 15 © AP Images; p. 19 NASA's Goddard Space Flight Center; p. 20 NASA; p. 21 NASA/Dmitri Gerondidakis; graphic elements cover, p. 1 (background) Perzeus/Shutterstock.com, pp. 2, 3, 22, 23 Visual Generation/Shutterstock.com, pp. 5, 9, 13, 18 Macrovector/Shutterstock.com, pp. 10, 12, 20 Oliver Hoffmann/Shutterstock.com.